..and it gets ZiGGiER every year !!!

★ SCIENCE NEWS ⚙
PROOF...THERE
IS INTELLIGENT
LIFE ON PLANET
EARTH

it's a ZiGGY WORLD

by Tom Wilson

Published by
Sheed and Ward, Inc. — New York
Subsidiary of Universal Press Syndicate
For American Greetings Corp. Cleveland, Ohio

...for YOU
my "ZiGGY" friend

...IT'S HARD TO BELIEVE THAT SOMEDAY THESE WILL BE CONSIDERED "THE GOOD OLE DAYS"!!

YOU REALLY KNOW YOU'RE A LOSER WHEN THE ONLY MAIL YOU GET IS ADDRESSED "OCCUPANT.".

YOUR PAY INCREASE WILL BECOME EFFECTIVE THE DAY YOU DO!!

THERE ARE SO MANY THINGS
THAT JUST DON'T MAKE SENSE..

...LIKE HOW COME USED BRICKS
ARE MORE EXPENSIVE THAN
NEW ONES...???

..AND WHY DOES IT COST MORE
TO HAVE YOUR PHONE NUMBER
UNLISTED??

Tom Wilson

TOO BAD MY NAME ISN'T "IRREGULAR" ...THEN ALL MY SHIRTS WOULD BE MONOGRAMMED!!

SHIRT SALE SLIGHTLY IMPERFECT

THIS IS YOUR WAKE-UP SERVICE, MR. ZIGGY...
...SORRY, BUT I OVERSLEPT !!
TomWilson

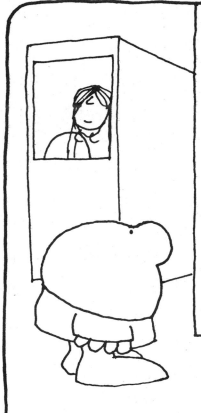

NOW SHOWING

NEW RELEASE OF
Snow White
and the
Seven Dwarfs

X-RATED

TELL US SIR... DO YOU THINK THE MAYOR'S NEW ANTI-CRIME CRUSADE IS RESTORING PEOPLE'S FAITH IN THE DOWNTOWN AREA??

...AND YOUR NEW TICKTO WATCH COMES WITH A TWO YEAR, UNCONDITIONAL GUARANTEE...

...not to explode, disintegrate, or contract Dutch Elm disease.

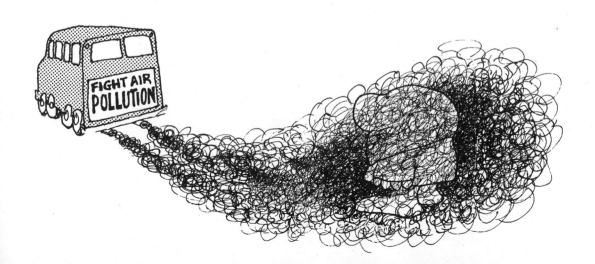

YOU'RE THE LAST PERSON I'M
EVER GONNA HOLD UP...
I'M SOB RETIRING AFTER 35 YEARS
...AND I WANNA SAY THANKS
FOR EVERYTHING...YOU'VE ALL
BEEN SO GENEROUS,
..SO SOB UNSELFISH...

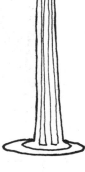

WHEN THE GOING GETS TOUGH... THE TOUGH GET GOING
... AND WHEN THE TOUGH GET GOING.. ..THE GOING GETS TOUGHER !!

QUICK DRYING PAINT

Tom Wilson

HANG IN THERE BABY!

LOVE is THE ANSWER

...i WONDER WHAT THE QUESTION WAS ??

Many of us are
more capable than
some of us...

..but none of us
are as capable as
all of us !!

MY PHILOSOPHY
IS A COMPROMISE
BETWEEN THE
BEST OF RADICAL
THINKING, AND
ESTABLISHMENT
THINKING...

...IT'S CALLED
OPEN-MINDED
UNCERTAINTY !!

IN THE GAME OF LIFE... IT'S NOT WHETHER YOU WIN OR LOSE THAT'S IMPORTANT...
IN THE LONG RUN IT'S WHETHER YOU MANAGE TO SURVIVE...

tomorrow is the first day of the rest of your life
...SURE HOPE IT'S BETTER THAN THE LAST DAY OF MY LIFE SO FAR....

ONE CONSOLING THING
ABOUT GETTING KICKED
FROM THE REAR...

...AT LEAST YOU KNOW THAT
YOU'RE OUT IN FRONT
OF SOMEBODY !!

Tom Wilson, creator of Ziggy, is a real-life Ziggy himself. He lives and works in Cleveland, Ohio.

Ziggy now stars on a complete line of greeting cards, posters and other such things produced by *American Greetings Corporation* available at all fine stores.